JESUS' SEVEN LAST WORDS

...oadcast

A
BACK TO THE BIBLE
PUBLICATION

Back to the Bible

Lincoln, Nebraska 68501

80,000 printed to date—1981
(5-0002—80M—31)
ISBN 0-8474-6502-0

Printed in the United States of America

Contents

Acknowledgements

I have preached on this subject over the years and have studied many books and been greatly helped. I especially want to acknowledge my debt to the writings of: Arthur W. Pink, Russell Bradley Jones, F. W. Boreham, W. M. Clow, F. W. Krummacher, James Stalker, Hubert Simpson and Marcus L. Loane.

—Warren W. Wiersbe
January, 1981

Chapter 1
"Father, Forgive Them"

On the day that Karl Marx died, March 14, 1883, his housekeeper came to him and said, "Tell me your last words, and I'll write them down." Marx replied, "Go on, get out! Last words are for fools who haven't said enough!"

Last words can be very revealing. P. T. Barnum said, as he was dying, "What were today's receipts?" Napoleon said, "Chief of the army!" The great Baptist preacher, Charles Spurgeon, said as his last words, "Jesus died for me." And John Wesley, the founder of Methodism, said, "The best of all is, God is with us."

In these studies we are considering the seven statements that our Lord made from the cross—His seven last words from the cross. These statements are very important to us, not only because of the Person who spoke them but also because of the place where they were said. When our Lord was doing His greatest work on earth, He was uttering some of His greatest words. These seven last words from the cross are windows that enable us to look into eternity and see the heart of God.

The first of these seven statements is found in Luke 23:33,34: "And when they were come to the place, which is called Calvary, there they crucified him, and the malefactors, one on the right hand, and the other on the left. Then said Jesus, Father, forgive them; for they know not what they do."

Sometimes it is very difficult for us to forgive people. How easy it is for us to harbor an unforgiving spirit. Someone hurts us, someone says something against us, and in our hearts we cannot forgive that person. Listen to this prayer, "Father, forgive them; for they know not what they do" (v. 34), and notice the wonders that are in this statement. If we grasp the wonders of this statement, I think it will enable us to forgive and to experience the joy that comes when we forgive.

The Address

First, there is the wonder of the address—"Father" (Luke 23:34). Our Lord Jesus addressed God three times when He was on the cross. His first statement was "Father, forgive them; for they know not what they do" (v. 34). And then the fourth statement was "My God, my God, why hast thou forsaken me?" (Matt. 27:46), and then that final statement was "Father, into thy hands I commend my spirit" (Luke 23:46). When our Lord *entered into* His suffering, when our Lord was *enduring* suffering, and when our Lord *emerged* victoriously from His suffering, He spoke to His Father in heaven. You see, nothing threatened His relationship with His Father.

I hear Christians say, "I can't talk to God! I can't pray! I don't believe anymore—after the way people have treated me!" Look at the way they treated the

6

Lord Jesus! His nation sinned against Him. His own disciples failed Him and fled. The Father was willing for the Son to suffer. And yet Jesus was able to look up and say, "Father." You see, He lived in fellowship with His Father. When He began His ministry, the Father said, "This is my beloved Son" (Matt. 3:17). They enjoyed a fellowship of love.

Perhaps you are hurting just now. You are saying, "I wonder if God really loves me." He does, He always will, and He is working out His purpose for you. When you can pray "Father," then you can receive from God the power, grace and help the Father has for you when you are suffering. I know it's not easy to suffer. Pain hurts. A broken heart hurts even worse than a broken arm. But when you can say "Father," then you are able to look up to heaven and know that the smile of God is upon you. The wonder of the address—"Father." If you want to be able to forgive others, here is the place to start—make sure you have a right relationship with your Father in heaven.

The Appeal

Second, there is the wonder of the appeal—"Father, forgive them" (Luke 23:34). The Greek New Testament indicates that our Lord repeated this prayer. He said several times, "Father, forgive them." As they laid Him on the cross on the ground, He said, "Father, forgive them." As they nailed His hands and His feet to that cross, He prayed again, "Father, forgive them." When they lifted that cross

7

and placed it in the hole in the ground, our Lord prayed, "Father, forgive them." As He was hanging there between heaven and earth, He was repeatedly praying, "Father, forgive them."

He could have prayed, "Father, judge them; Father, bring punishment upon them." He could have called for legions of angels to deliver Him, but He did not do it. Many times you and I have wanted to bring down fire from heaven on somebody, and we've prayed, "O Father, judge them; Father, hurt them." But our Lord prayed from a heart of love, "Father, forgive them."

Fulfilling God's Word

Why did He pray this prayer? For one thing, He was fulfilling the Word of God. In Isaiah 53:12 (the great Calvary chapter of the Old Testament) we read these words: "Therefore will I divide him a portion with the great, and he shall divide the spoil with the strong; because he hath poured out his soul unto death: and he was numbered with the transgressors; and he bare the sin of many, and made intercession for the transgressors." Our Lord Jesus Christ prayed for those who were sinning because He was fulfilling the Word of God.

Practicing His Message

Second, He was practicing the very message that He preached. He preached forgiveness. He told people in His messages, "Now, if you don't forgive

8

from your heart, God cannot forgive you." This does not mean that forgiveness is based upon our own good works. No, but it does mean that if my heart is unwilling to forgive you, it is in no condition to come and ask God for forgiveness for myself.

You must remember that all of this happened during the reign of Caesar during the time of the Roman Empire. Did you know that the Romans worshiped revenge? Revenge was one of their gods. Our Lord Jesus Christ did not worship revenge, nor should we. He prayed, "Father, forgive them"; in so doing He fulfilled the Word, and He practiced His own message of forgiveness.

Purpose of His Death

And, of course, this was the purpose of His death. Our Lord Jesus was on the cross because God does forgive sinners. That's the message of the gospel. You and I don't have to go around with the weight and the burden of sin. We don't have to carry the guilt of sin. We can be forgiven!

In Luke 5:20, it is recorded that our Lord said to the paralytic, "Thy sins be forgiven thee." He said to the woman of the street who was brought to Him, "Thy sins are forgiven. . . . Go in peace" (7:48,50). Forgiveness is what the cross is all about; and of course forgiveness is not cheap, it is very expensive. It cost Jesus Christ His life.

You and I will have no problem forgiving others if we are right in our relationship with our Father and if we will obey the Word of God, remembering that

9

we have been forgiven. Those who do not forgive others tear down the bridge on which they have to walk themselves. Perhaps you argue, "But, Pastor Wiersbe, you have no idea how other people treated me." Well, I have some idea of how they treated the Lord Jesus, and yet He was able to say, "Father, forgive them; for they know not what they do" (23:34). The wonder of the address, and the wonder of the appeal.

The Argument

There is a third wonder here—the wonder of the argument, "For they know not what they do" (Luke 23:34). Our Lord not only prayed for forgiveness for His enemies, but our Lord argued on their behalf! It is as though He stood as a lawyer and said to His Father, "Let Me give You a reason why You should forgive them."

This statement has been greatly misunderstood. This statement does not mean that everybody is automatically forgiven. Nor does it mean that ignorance brings forgiveness. Ignorance is no excuse in the sight of the law.

I recall one day driving in the city of Chicago and making a left turn. Before long I saw behind me that flashing light. The policeman pulled me over and said, "Sir, you made an illegal turn." Now I had made that turn many times, but they had changed the law and had put up a "No Left Turn" sign, and I hadn't noticed it. I said, "Well, Officer, I'm sorry, I did not know." Do you know what he said to me?

"Sir, that doesn't make any difference." Ignorance is no excuse in the sight of the law.

Ignorant of His Person

Then what was our Lord saying? Of what were they ignorant? Well, they were ignorant of His Person. They mocked Him as a prophet. They said, "Prophesy, tell us who struck you" (see Luke 22:64). They mocked Him as the king—they put a robe on Him, gave Him a scepter and a crown of thorns. They laughed at His claim that He was the Son of God, the Christ. "If you are the Christ, come down from the cross," they challenged Him (see 23:37). They were ignorant of His Person. We know who Jesus is. We have a complete New Testament, we have 2000 years of church history. We know who Jesus is—the very Son of God Himself.

Ignorant of Their Own Actions

They were ignorant of their own actions. They didn't realize that what they were doing was a fulfillment of the Word of God. They parted His garments (Luke 23:34), and that fulfilled Psalm 22:18. They gave Him vinegar to drink (Luke 23:36), and that fulfilled Psalm 69:21. He was crucified with the transgressors (Luke 23:33), and that fulfilled Isaiah 53:12.

Ignorant of Their Sin

Most of all, they were ignorant of the enormity of

their own sins. They did not realize what great sinners they were. In the Old Testament, the Jewish Law made provision for sins of ignorance. The sin offering described in Leviticus 4 was for sins of ignorance that had been discovered. Jesus was saying, "Father, My people don't understand; they are ignorant. I am dying for them. They know not what they do; I know what I'm doing—I'm dying in their behalf. Now, forgive them." The wonder of the argument.

The Answer

What did this prayer bring about as far as God's will was concerned? Look at the wonder of the answer. What was God's answer? Judgment did not fall. God still sent His message of salvation to the Jews. In Acts 3:17 the Apostle Peter said to the Jewish leaders, "I wot [know] that through ignorance ye did it." The Apostle Paul himself, in I Timothy 1:13, said, "I did it ignorantly in unbelief." God was patient with Israel, and God was patient with Saul of Tarsus. Many people in Jerusalem did come to know Christ as Saviour; and, of course, Saul was saved and became the great Apostle Paul.

You see, God does not judge sin immediately. God in His mercy postpones His judgment because His Son prayed, "Father, forgive them; for they know not what they do" (Luke 23:34). You and I are living in a day of grace, not a day of judgment—a day when God is seeking to reconcile lost sinners to Himself. Yes, this is a wonderful prayer, isn't it? And

12

God answered that prayer. He can forgive you today if you will trust Christ.

Charles Wesley wrote in one of his hymns:

> Five bleeding wounds He bears,
> Received on Calvary;
> They pour effectual prayers,
> They strongly plead for me,
> "Forgive him, O forgive," they cry,
> "Nor let that ransomed sinner die."

"Father, forgive them; for they know not what they do."

Chapter 2
"With Me in Paradise"

Whenever a person trusts Jesus Christ and is converted, it is an amazing experience. It is amazing because a miracle takes place. The spiritually dead sinner is raised to eternal life. He is brought from darkness to light. He experiences a new birth, he receives the divine nature within. This is the experience of every converted sinner who turns to Jesus Christ and trusts Him as Saviour.

But the circumstances that surround some conversions are much more marvelous than others. When I trusted Christ as my Saviour, I was standing at the back of a high school auditorium listening to an evangelist preach the gospel. I did not raise a hand or walk an aisle; I simply opened my heart to Christ and I was saved. These circumstances were quite different from the conversion of the Apostle Paul (see Acts 9:1-8). He saw a light! He heard a voice! He saw the Lord Jesus! Each conversion is amazing, but the circumstances of some conversions are more amazing than others. When you consider the conversion of the thief on the cross, you have to admit that it really was amazing.

"And the people stood beholding. And the rulers also with them derided him, saying, He saved others; let him save himself, if he be Christ, the chosen

14

of God. And the soldiers also mocked him, coming to him, and offering him vinegar, and saying, If thou be the king of the Jews, save thyself. And a super-scription also was written over him in letters of Greek, and Latin, and Hebrew, This Is The King Of The Jews. And one of the malefactors which were hanged railed at him, saying, If thou be the Christ, save thyself and us. But the other answering rebuked him, saying, Dost not thou fear God, see-ing thou art in the same condemnation? And we indeed justly; for we receive the due reward of our deeds: but this man hath done nothing amiss. And he said unto Jesus, Lord, remember me when thou comest into thy kingdom. And Jesus said unto him, Verily I say unto thee, To day shalt thou be with me in paradise" (Luke 23:35-43).

This was our Lord's second statement from the cross. The first statement was "Father, forgive them; for they know not what they do" (v. 34). Our Lord first prayed for His enemies. In His second statement He turned to a repentant sinner and gave him the assurance that he was going to heaven. Consider the amazing aspects of this man's conver-sion.

Amazing Situation

First of all, you cannot help but notice the amaz-ing situation at Calvary. When they crucified our Lord Jesus, they put Him between two thieves. They could have put the two thieves together. In fact, that would have been the natural thing to do.

We get the impression that these two thieves were partners in crime, and certainly it would have been a good thing for the soldiers to put these two friends together. Instead, they put the Lord Jesus between the two thieves. This was an amazing situation.

Fulfillment of Prophecy

To begin with, it was the fulfillment of prophecy. We have noticed in Isaiah 53:12 that "He was numbered with the transgressors": "And with him they crucify two thieves; the one on his right hand, and the other on his left. And the scripture was fulfilled, which saith, And he was numbered with the transgressors" (Mark 15:27,28).

Remember that at Calvary not only was the hand of man at work but also the hand of God. Man was fulfilling the plan of God, doing it freely, responsibly, but fulfilling Old Testament prophecy. The Lord Jesus was numbered with the transgressors. He was *born* for the transgressors: "Thou shalt call his name Jesus: for he shall save his people from their sins" (Matt. 1:21). He *lived* for the transgressors: "Even as the Son of man came not to be ministered unto, but to minister, and to give his life a ransom for many" (20:28). He died *with* them, and He died *for* them. So that amazing situation began with the fulfillment of prophecy.

God's Gracious Providence

But there is something else about that amazing situation. Our Lord Jesus was between the thieves because God was working out His gracious providence. The word "providence" means "foreknowledge" or "seeing beforehand." God does see beforehand. There were no accidents in the life of the Lord Jesus—only appointments. It was not accidental that the Lord Jesus was between these two thieves. This was the working of the gracious providence of God. You see, *both* of the thieves could hear Him pray, "Father, forgive them; for they know not what they do" (Luke 23:34). The Holy Spirit of God could take that prayer and speak to their hearts: "Here is One who forgives and who prays that others might be forgiven."

Because those thieves were on either side of the Lord Jesus, they could see the title that was on the cross. When you study the harmony of the Gospels, you find that this title read: "This is Jesus of Nazareth, the King of the Jews." It was written in three languages, and the thieves probably knew at least two of those languages. That title was written by Pilate. It was perhaps the first gospel tract ever written, and it hung over the head of the Lord Jesus. Those two thieves, as they looked at each other, had to look at the Lord Jesus! As they looked at the Lord Jesus, they had to see that title—and that title told them who He is. He is Jesus, which means "Saviour." He is Jesus of Nazareth. He came from a despised and a rejected place, identified with the outcasts. He is the King of the Jews—He is a Saviour who has a kingdom! And so, in reading this title, they could get the message of the gospel.

He is the Saviour—He is the Saviour of lost

sinners. He has a kingdom, and He is the King of the Jews.

Also, both thieves could hear the crowd as it railed upon Him. The soldiers mocked Him: "If thou be the king of the Jews, save thyself" (v. 37). And the people and the rulers (meaning the religious rulers) mocked Him. Listen to what they said: "He saved others" (v. 35). That must have been good news! I can imagine one thief, at least, saying to himself, "If He saved others, then He can save me." Pilate put that superscription on the cross to quiet his own conscience, but that superscription was used of God to win a lost soul. The soldiers and the rulers mocked the Lord Jesus, but God used their mockery to win a lost soul. How amazing is the working of the gracious providence of God!

Each of the thieves had access to the Lord Jesus. It wasn't as though they had to go far away—He was there between them. Because they were crucified together, the thieves called back and forth to each other, and as they did, they had to look at Jesus. As they looked upon Him, they saw something different about Him, and they had access to Him.

God still works in His providence to set up situations for people to be saved. No one is ever saved by accident. This is the way God works. God sets up the situation to give you an opportunity to trust Jesus Christ and to believe and be saved. "The Lord is . . . not willing that any should perish" (II Pet. 3:9). "God . . . will have all men to be saved" (I Tim. 2:3,4). One of the great tragedies today is the tragedy of people missing their opportunities to

18

trust the Saviour. The amazing situation—Jesus in the midst.

Amazing Supplication

Notice the amazing supplication. The prayer that the one thief prayed is truly one of the amazing prayers in the Bible. Look at what he had to confess when he prayed this prayer. He admitted that he feared God—he was not an agnostic, he was not an atheist, he was not irreligious. He admitted his guilt. "We are here justly" (see Luke 23:41). He admitted he deserved this punishment. He admitted that Jesus Christ was innocent, and he admitted that there was a life after death. That's an amazing confession from this thief on the cross.

Do you believe that there is a life after death? Are you prepared for it? If you were to die now, where would you go? Do you believe that Jesus Christ is the Lord of paradise? Do you believe that you deserve judgment, that you are a guilty sinner? Do you believe there is a God and that you are going to have to answer to Him?

I'm also amazed at the courage this man showed when he spoke to the Lord Jesus. Nobody else was asking Jesus for salvation! The priests and the rulers were mocking Christ, and yet this thief dared to believe on Jesus. The crowd was opposing Him, the soldiers were laughing at Him, this thief's own friend (and I'm assuming these two were partners in crime) was mocking the Lord Jesus. Some people don't want to trust the Lord Jesus because they are afraid of people. Here was a man who had courage. He dared to defy the rulers and the priests and the soldiers and his own friend when he trusted the Lord Jesus!

Just stop to think of how little this man really understood about Jesus. Let me list the facts. "Jesus" means "Saviour." Jesus had a kingdom. Jesus was innocent. Jesus came from Nazareth, and He saved others.

I hear people say, "Well, I'd like to be saved, but I want to understand more about it." My friend, this thief didn't understand a great deal. But what he did understand led him to the Saviour. He saw the Lord Jesus rejected, abused, dying, weak. Would you trust someone in that condition? I could see him trusting the Lord Jesus if Christ had done a miracle. But Jesus didn't do a miracle. Jesus was forsaken, mocked, laughed at, and yet this thief dared to trust Him.

We invite you to trust a Saviour who is risen and glorified, who is seated upon the throne of the universe. There is no problem trusting that kind of a Saviour! The thief didn't have a great deal of knowledge, did he? He didn't see a beautiful sight as he looked at the Lord Jesus; and yet the thief believed and was saved. I really believe that this man's faith ranks very high in the Word of God. We have a completed Bible. We have the Holy Spirit of God witnessing to people. We have the Church bearing witness in this dark world. And yet many people still will not trust the Saviour. I say this man's salvation certainly speaks to our own hearts today: the amazing situation, the amazing supplication.

Amazing Salvation

There is a third aspect of his conversion that is amazing—not only the amazing situation and the amazing supplication but also the amazing salvation.

The Lord Jesus Christ came "to seek and to save that which was lost" (Luke 19:10). You cannot save people who don't know that they are lost. One of the problems today is that people will not admit that they are lost. People are lost sheep, and they don't realize it. They are traveling with the flock, and the flock is going in the wrong direction. They are on the broad road that leads to destruction. They are lost coins—they have value, but what good is that value if it is lost? They are lost sons, lost daughters, who turn their backs on their fathers and have gone into the far country.

This thief was a lost man who knew he was lost. He was a condemned man who knew he was condemned. Because of this, he turned to the Lord Jesus and said, "Lord, remember me when thou comest into thy kingdom" (23:42). And Jesus gave to him an amazing salvation: "Verily I say unto thee, To day shalt thou be with me in paradise" (v. 43).

Wholly by Grace

What are the characteristics of this salvation that make it so amazing? To begin with, this salvation

21

was wholly by grace. This man did not deserve to be saved, and he admitted it. He said, "[We are] in the same condemnation[.] And we indeed justly; for we receive the due reward of our deeds" (Luke 23:40,41). He admitted that he did not deserve to be saved.

The first man that God made became a thief: Adam and Eve took from the tree and disobeyed God. The first Adam became a thief and was cast out of Paradise. The last Adam, Jesus Christ, turned to a thief and said, "To day shalt thou be with me in paradise" (v. 43). That, my friend, is grace. God, in His mercy, does not give us what we do deserve—hell; and God, in His grace gives us what we don't deserve—heaven.

This thief could not earn his salvation. I have had people tell me that in order to go to heaven you have to keep the Ten Commandments. The dying thief did not have time to keep the Ten Commandments. Someone else says, "In order to get to heaven, you have to go through some religious ritual." This man didn't have opportunity for any religious ritual. Let's not complicate salvation. This man's conversion was wholly by the grace of God. The man did not deserve it, the man did not earn it, the man simply received it by faith.

Wherever you have faith, you have to have grace; wherever you have law, you have to have works. This man could not work for his salvation; all he could do was receive it as a gracious gift from God.

Have you received salvation as a gracious gift from God? Are you bragging about your religion?

Are you saying, "I say so many prayers, I attend so many meetings, I do so many good works." If that's your situation, you may not be saved; because when we are saved by grace, we don't brag about it. "For by grace are ye saved through faith; and that not of yourselves: it is the gift of God: Not of works, lest any man should boast" (Eph. 2:8,9).

Certain and Secure

There is something else about this amazing salvation—it was secure. It was not a "hope-so" salvation, not a "guess-so" salvation. "Amen, I say unto thee." That's what Jesus said to the man— "Verily [amen] I say unto thee" (Luke 23:43). How did this man know his salvation was secure? Because Jesus told him so. You may say, "But Jesus is not here to tell me—I don't hear His voice audibly." But you have His Word! The same word that we have in the Scriptures is secure and certain. "For ever, O Lord, thy word is settled in heaven" (Ps. 119:89). Jesus Himself said to this man, "To day shalt thou be with me in paradise" (Luke 23:43). His salvation was certain, and it was secure.

I have had people say to me, "Well, you won't know if you're saved until you die." That's just a little bit too close for me! That's taking a chance. I want to know *before I die* that I'm going to heaven. This man did. This undeserving sinner, this thief, knew he was going to heaven. How did he know it? Jesus told him so.

We sing that little song, "Jesus loves me! this I

23

know, For the Bible tells me so." I like to sing, "Jesus *saves* me! this I know, For the Bible tells me so."

Personal

There is a third characteristic to this salvation. It was wholly of grace, it was certain and secure, and it was personal. Jesus spoke to this man personally: "Verily I say unto *thee*" (Luke 23:43).

You see, God loves us personally. I know John 3:16 says, "God so loved the world." Paul wrote: "[He] loved me, and gave himself for me" (Gal. 2:20). The Lord Jesus Christ died for us personally. God's love is shown to us personally, and God saves us personally. God doesn't deal with us as part of a crowd. God does not save people *en masse*. God saves people individually, one by one. This was a personal salvation given to this thief.

Present

It was a personal salvation, and it was a present salvation: "To day shalt thou be with me in paradise" (Luke 23:43). Notice that word "today." The man had said, "Lord, remember me when thou comest into thy kingdom" (v. 42). It was as though the thief said, "Sometime in the future, you are going to have a kingdom. Please remember me when that happens." But Jesus said, "Why wait until the future? I'll give you salvation right now— today."

24

Salvation is not a process. You don't get a little bit saved today, a little more saved next week, a little more saved next year. Salvation is an instantaneous spiritual experience by the power of God when you put your faith in Jesus Christ. "To day shalt thou be with me in paradise" (v. 43). A personal, present salvation.

Centered in Christ

I notice also that this salvation was centered in the Lord Jesus Christ. "To day shalt thou be with me in paradise" (Luke 23:43). Salvation means being related to Jesus Christ. Jesus Christ was identified with this man in condemnation, and this man was identified with Jesus Christ in salvation. That's what the cross is all about. Salvation is not centered in Moses, or keeping the Law. It is not centered in John the Baptist. It is not centered in some preacher, some church or some revered person from the past. Salvation is centered in Jesus Christ.

This thief could not turn to the other thief and say, "Remember me when thou comest into thy kingdom," because his friend did not have a kingdom. This thief could not turn to one of the soldiers and say, "Remember me when you come into your kingdom." He could not turn to one of the religious leaders or to the priests—they could do nothing for him. He had to turn to Jesus Christ.

Have you ever turned to Jesus Christ and asked Him to save you? This was a salvation wholly by grace, certain and secure, personal, present and centered in Jesus Christ.

Glorious

Notice also that this salvation was glorious. "To day shalt thou be with me in paradise" (Luke 23:43). All the man had hoped for was to share in some kind of a future kingdom about which he knew very little. Jesus said, "I'm going to give you far more than you ever asked for or hoped for—you're going to be with Me in paradise." The Apostle Paul, in II Corinthians 12, tells us that paradise is the third heaven, where God dwells. Jesus said to the thief, "You are going to be with Me in a place of glory and praise where there will be no pain, no sorrow, no tears and no death."

You may say, "Well, I'm going to be like that thief—I'm going to wait until the very last minute, and then I'm going to trust Jesus as my Saviour." If you say that, you have two great problems to solve. Number one: You don't know when that "last minute" is going to be. Would you sign a paper right now saying, "I will postpone the salvation of my soul until just a few minutes before I die"? Of course not, because you don't know when your last minute will come. But the big problem is this: The dying thief was not saved at the last opportunity he had—he was saved the first opportunity he had! We have no reason to believe that this man had heard Jesus preach before they met at Calvary. When he had his first opportunity, the thief trusted in Jesus Christ.

26

The only difference between you and this thief is this—he got caught! You haven't gotten caught yet, but one day you will. Trust the Saviour today!

> The dying thief rejoiced to see
> That fountain in his day,
> And there may I, though vile as he,
> Wash all my sins away.

"To day shalt thou be with me in paradise."

Chapter 3
"Behold Thy Son! . . . Behold Thy Mother!"

"Greater love hath no man than this, that a man lay down his life for his friends" (John 15:13). Our Lord Jesus said that, and as we have been looking at the words He spoke from the cross, we realize how great His love is. He not only died for His friends, He also died for His enemies. "While we were yet sinners, Christ died for us" (Rom. 5:8).

"Now there stood by the cross of Jesus his mother, and his mother's sister, Mary the wife of Cleophas, and Mary Magdalene. When Jesus therefore saw his mother, and the disciple standing by, whom he loved, he saith unto his mother, Woman, behold thy son! Then saith he to the disciple, Behold thy mother! And from that hour that disciple took her unto his own home" (John 19:25-27). That disciple, of course, was John, who wrote the Gospel of John and bore witness of these things.

If you and I had been in Jerusalem that Passover afternoon when Jesus was crucified, I wonder how near the cross we would have stood. It is one thing to sing, "Jesus, keep me near the cross," and it is quite another thing to actually stay near the cross. The four Roman soldiers were there, but they were there because of duty. The four women were there, with the Apostle John; but they were not there because of duty. They were there out of devotion; they loved the Lord Jesus. Mary, His mother, was there; Mary Magdalene was there; Salome (His mother's sister) was there; and Mary, the wife of Cleophas, was there; and John was there.

We use the phrase "near the cross" quite often. It has become one of our evangelical clichés. We've prayed, "O Lord, keep me near the cross," and we sing about standing near the cross. What does it really mean to be near the cross of Jesus?

Obviously we are not talking about literal geography. The cross is gone, and you and I are not able to go outside the city wall of Jerusalem and stand near the cross. We are talking about a spiritual position; we are talking about a special relationship to Jesus Christ.

This third word from the cross helps us to understand what it means to be near the cross. Perhaps the best thing we can do is just talk to the people who were there. Let's interview Mary Magdalene, Salome, the two Marys and John and find out what it really means to be near the cross of Jesus Christ. What did the cross mean to each of these persons?

A Place of Redemption

Let's begin with Mary Magdalene. She is listed last in John 19:25, but I want to start with her. If you had walked up to Mary Magdalene that afternoon and said, "Mary Magdalene, you are standing near

29

the cross. What does it mean to you?" I think she would have answered, "The cross to me is a place of redemption."

Mary Magdalene had been delivered by the Lord Jesus Christ. It is unfortunate that some Bible students and some preachers have confused the woman in Luke 7 with Mary Magdalene. Luke 7:36-50 records an event in which our Lord was having dinner with a Pharisee when a woman of the streets came in—a woman of very unsavory reputation. She worshiped the Lord Jesus and anointed Him with expensive perfume. Many people have equated this woman with Mary Magdalene, but this is not true. We do not know this woman's name.

Mary Magdalene is mentioned in Luke 8:2 as a woman out of whom Jesus had cast seven demons. (This same fact is recorded in Mark 16:9.) Mary Magdalene not only was at the cross, but also early on the morning of the resurrection she came to Christ's tomb. Mary Magdalene had been in bondage to Satan. I personally cannot conceive of what it would be like to be possessed by one demon let alone seven demons! We do not know what they made her do, but she was in terrible, terrible bondage. Now before we judge her, let's remember that Ephesians 2:1-3 makes it very clear that every unsaved person is walking "according to the prince of the power of the air, the spirit that now worketh in the children of disobedience." The demonic forces are at work in the lives of unbelievers today, and these demonic forces would like to oppress the minds and distress the hearts of God's people as well. Satan was at work in Mary Magdalene's life, and then Jesus delivered her from those demonic powers.

Whenever I think of deliverance, I think of Acts 26:18. God spoke these words to Paul to tell him what his ministry of the gospel was going to be: "To open their eyes, and to turn them from darkness to light, and from the power of Satan unto God, that they may receive forgiveness of sins, and inheritance among them which are sanctified by faith that is in me." When you trust the Lord Jesus Christ, these marvelous changes take place in your life. You go from darkness to light—from mental darkness, moral darkness and spiritual darkness into the wonderful light of the gospel of Jesus Christ. You go from the power of Satan to the power of God. God begins to control and to use your life. You go from guilt to forgiveness, and you go from poverty to wealth as an heir of God through faith in Jesus Christ. This is what Jesus did for Mary Magdalene.

This miracle of redemption is a costly thing. When Jesus delivered Mary Magdalene from the power of the Wicked One, it cost Him something. Standing there at the cross, Mary saw the price being paid. You see, Jesus had to die that we might be redeemed. For me to move out of the darkness into the light, He had to move from the light into the darkness. For me to be delivered from Satan to God, Jesus Christ had to be forsaken by God. For me to be delivered from guilt to forgiveness, Jesus had to be made sin for me. For Him to make me

31

rich, He had to become the poorest of the poor. No wonder Mary was standing there at the cross. No wonder she was there when Jesus was buried. No wonder she was early at the tomb on resurrection morning. Mary Magdalene had experienced redemption. Standing near the cross, Mary said, "The cross to me is a place of redemption."

Is the cross in your life a place of redemption? Can you say, "I have trusted Jesus Christ, and He has moved me from darkness to light, from the power of Satan to the power of God, from the guilt of sin to forgiveness, from poverty to an inheritance through faith in Him"? If this is not true in your life, then you are missing all that Jesus died to give you. Ask Him to save you, and then you can take your stand near the cross, a place of redemption.

A Place of Rebuke

The second person I'd like us to talk to is Salome. Salome was an interesting person. She was Mary's sister, the mother of James and John, and the wife of Zebedee. We remember her as the woman who came with her sons asking for thrones. In Matthew 20:20-28 we have the account. Salome and James and John came to Jesus and said, "We want to ask something of you." Jesus said, "What do you want?" They had heard Him say that the apostles were going to judge the 12 tribes of Israel, that they were going to sit on thrones; and they wanted to be sure they had good seats! They said to Jesus, "We would like to have the thrones on your right hand

and on your left." Jesus said, "Are you able to drink the cup I'm going to drink? Are you able to be baptized with the baptism I'm going to experience?" Very glibly they said, "Yes we are." He said, "You will; indeed, you will." Of course, James was the first of the apostles to be martyred. John was the last of the apostles to die, and he went through great persecution and suffering before he was called home.

"Salome, we want to ask you, what kind of a place is the cross? You are standing near the cross. What does it mean to you?" I think she would have answered, "The cross to me is a place of rebuke. I stand here rebuked, because I was so selfish. I wanted my two sons to have the places of honor. I wanted them at the right hand and the left hand of the Lord Jesus Christ; now I stand here seeing Him not on a throne but on a cross, and I'm ashamed of myself."

Indeed, she might well be ashamed of herself—as all of us should be when we pray selfishly! Her prayer was a selfish prayer. "I want something for my sons; I don't care what it costs. I want it!" Her prayer was born of pride, not of humility. Did these two men deserve thrones? Thrones are not given carelessly; you have to earn them. Salome had forgotten the cost of true reward. There is no crown without a cross; there is no wearing of the crown without the drinking of the cup. Even our Lord Jesus Christ Himself did not return to the throne except by way of the cross.

The cross to Salome was a place of rebuke. How much we need to sing,

> When I survey the wondrous cross
> On which the Prince of glory died,
> My richest gain I count but loss,
> And pour contempt on all my pride.
>
> Forbid it, Lord, that I should boast,
> Save in the death of Christ, my God;
> All the vain things that charm me most—
> I sacrifice them to His blood.

Sometimes the most selfish things that we do come because of our wrong praying. No Christian rises any higher than his praying. Salome did not bring her prayers to the cross. As a consequence, her praying was selfish, earthly, proud and ignorant. She did not realize the price she was going to pay.

God will answer prayer, but we must be sure we can pay the price. James did pay a price—he was martyred. John did pay a price—he had to suffer and was persecuted. Salome looked upon the cross as a place of rebuke, and I confess to you that many times as I have contemplated the cross I have been rebuked, because my praying has been selfish, my praying has been proud. God has looked upon me and said, "Are you willing to drink the cup?" "Oh no, Lord, I want the answer to prayer." "But you must drink the cup. Are you willing to be baptized with the baptism of suffering?" "No, God, I just want the blessing, not the suffering!" Salome says to each of us, "The cross is a place of rebuke."

God delights in honoring His servants and His people. One day we are going to share in His eternal glory. But before the glory there has to be the suffering. "The God of all grace, who hath called us unto his eternal glory by Christ Jesus, after that ye have suffered a while" (I Pet. 5:10). Mary Magdalene told us that the cross is a place of redemption. Have you been redeemed? Salome told us that the cross is a place of rebuke. Perhaps as we stand near the cross, God rebukes our selfishness, pride and desire for glory without suffering.

A Place of Reward

Now we want to look at Mary and at John—Mary, the mother of our Lord Jesus, and John, the disciple whom Jesus loved. If you had stood by Mary at Calvary and asked her, "What does it mean for you to be near the cross?" I think she would have replied, "The cross to me is a place of reward."

It is interesting to note that we find Mary at the beginning of the Gospel of John and at the end of the Gospel of John. We find her in John 2 and in John 19, but the two incidents are in contrast. In John 2, Mary is attending a wedding and is involved in the joys of a feast. In John 19 she is involved in the sorrows of a funeral. In John 2 the Lord Jesus Christ displayed His power. He manifested His glory and turned the water into wine. But in John 19 our Lord Jesus Christ died in weakness and in shame. He could have exercised His power and delivered Himself, but had He done so, He would not have completed the work of salvation. He did not come to save Himself, He came to save us.

In John 2 we find Mary speaking, but in John 19 Mary is silent. Her silence is interesting; in fact, it is very important. We expect her to say something in John 2. They had run out of wine, and this was a social disgrace back in Jesus' day. (In fact, I read somewhere that a person could be fined for inviting people to a feast and not having sufficient wine.) Mary came to Jesus and said, "They have no wine." He met the need out of His gracious heart of love.

But in John 19, Mary is silent. I believe the one person who could have rescued Jesus from the cross was His mother, Mary! All Mary would have had to do was to walk up to those Roman soldiers and say, "I am His mother; I understand Him better than anyone else. What He says is not true; therefore, would you deliver Him?" Had Mary given this kind of witness, she could have saved the Lord Jesus, but she kept quiet. Do you know why she kept quiet? She could not lie. As she stood there by the cross, her silence was testimony that Jesus Christ is the Son of God. If anybody knows a son, certainly it is his mother. If Jesus Christ were not what He claimed to be, Mary could have saved Him. She kept silent, and her silence to me is an eloquent testimony that the Jesus Christ we worship is God—God the Son come in human flesh.

The cross was a place of reward for Mary. In what sense? In the sense that the Lord Jesus Christ did not ignore her but rewarded her by sharing His beloved disciple with her. Mary is to be honored, but she is not to be worshiped. We are told in the Gospel of Luke that Mary herself said she rejoiced in God her Saviour (Luke 1:47). Mary was saved by faith like any other sinner. Elisabeth did not say to her, "Blessed art thou *above* women." Elisabeth said, "Blessed art thou *among* women" (v. 42). We do bless Mary, because she suffered in order to bring the Saviour into the world.

Simeon had said to her, "A sword shall pierce through thy own soul also" (2:35). She experienced the climax of that suffering at the cross. When she was discovered with child, she began to suffer shame and reproach. She was misunderstood. People gossiped about her. She was married to Joseph, a poor carpenter, and lived in poverty. She gave birth to the Lord Jesus in a lowly stable. Then they had to flee from Bethlehem and escape the sword, and yet some innocent children died because of her baby. I wonder how Mary felt about that. She rejoiced that her child was delivered, but she must have felt the sword in her own soul when she heard that other innocent children had died.

When our Lord Jesus was a youth, He said to her, "Don't you know I must be about my Father's business?" (see v. 49). This began an experience of separation, a growing separation. At times Mary did not really understand Him. The sword was going through her own soul! The psalmist said it so eloquently in Psalm 69:8: "I am become a stranger unto my brethren, and an alien unto my mother's children." The sword was going through Mary's soul.

At the cross, Mary suffered because He died. She

suffered because of the way He died—on a cross, numbered with the transgressors. She suffered because of where He died—in public, with all sorts of people going by. It was such a cosmopolitan crowd that Pilate wrote the declaration for the cross in three different languages! Our Lord was not crucified in a corner somewhere! Openly, publicly, shamefully He was crucified! And there Mary stood, feeling the sword go through her soul.

But Jesus saw her, and Jesus assured her of His love. He always does this. You may be going through a Calvary experience. You may be standing by and suffering intensely because of something that has happened. I want you to know that the Lord Jesus Christ always assures us of His love. He said to her, "Woman [a title of respect], behold thy son!" (John 19:26). Was He speaking about Himself? I don't think so; I think He was talking about John. Then He said to John, "Behold thy mother!" (v. 27). What was He doing? He was establishing a new relationship. He was saying to Mary, "I am going to go back to heaven. Because of this, you and I must have a whole new relationship. But in order to give peace to your heart, in order to heal up your broken heart where the sword has pierced so deeply, I'm giving you John." He assured her of His love as He took His choice disciple and made him Mary's son. The Lord Jesus felt her sorrow, He knew her loneliness, and He rewarded her by giving to her the disciple whom He loved so dearly.

I read somewhere that the longest will ever probated was made up of four big volumes. There were

95,940 words in it! The shortest will on record is recorded in Great Britain, and it has only three words to it: "All for mother."

Jesus did not have any earthly possessions to give to anybody. The soldiers had gambled for his clothes and had taken them away. What could He give to Mary? He gave John to Mary. From that very hour John took her into his own house (v. 27). To Mary the cross was a place of reward. Ultimately God rewards those who have suffered.

A Place of Responsibility

And now we must speak to John. "John, what does it mean to you to be near the cross?" I think John would answer, "It is a place of responsibility." Our Lord Jesus reigned from the cross. He was in control. He was giving the orders. He was directing His own followers and His loved ones. He restored John. John had forsaken Him and fled. All the disciples had done this. The Shepherd had been smitten, and the sheep had scattered. But John came back to the cross. He was restored and forgiven!

You and I may stray, we may disobey, we may even deny our Lord, but we can come back. John came back to the cross. That was not the safest place to stand or the easiest place to stand. I have watched people die, but not in that kind of a situation. It took courage and love for John to come back. The Lord Jesus restored John, and it was John who one day wrote: "If we confess our sins, he is faithful and just to forgive us our sins, and to cleanse us from all unrighteousness" (I John 1:9).

Jesus not only restored John, but He also honored him. He said, "John, you are going to take My place. I will no longer be on earth to watch over My earthly mother, Mary, so you are going to take My place. You are going to take My mother, and you are going to be a son to her."

The interesting thing is this—all of us are taking His place! He said, following His resurrection, "As my Father hath sent me, even so send I you" (John 20:21). You and I represent Jesus Christ to others. John was to love Mary, because he would be taking our Lord's place in Mary's life. You and I are to love others the way the Lord Jesus has loved us. John was the disciple whom Jesus loved, and John was the disciple who loved the Lord Jesus. It is interesting to note in the latter chapters of the Gospel of John how John showed his love for the Lord Jesus.

In John 13:23 we read that John leaned on Jesus' breast—learned His secrets. Love is always close to the heart. In John 19:26 we learn that he stood at the cross. It is one thing to lean on Jesus' breast privately in the upper room, but it is quite something else to stand publicly by the cross. But love always stands and suffers. John 20:2 tells us that John ran to the sepulchre. He recognized Jesus and said, "It is the Lord" (21:7). Love always recognizes the beloved one. Then love followed (v. 21). Jesus said, "Follow me," and John began to follow the Lord Jesus. Finally, love testified (v. 24). John said,

"I am testifying of these things—I saw them, I know that they are true."

The cross is a place of responsibility. If you and I have come to the cross, we have a big responsibility—the responsibility of loving the Lord Jesus and then living for the Lord Jesus and loving others. The Christian life is not an easy life, but it is a wonderful life. I believe the Christian life is a lot easier than a sinful life! "Near the cross"—that's where He wants us to be. It is a place of redemption. If you have never trusted the Lord Jesus, you can be redeemed. Just come to the cross by faith and trust Him. "Near the cross" is a place of rebuke. All of our pride and our selfishness just fades away as we stand at the cross and see the Lord Jesus suffering for us. "Near the cross" is a place of reward. "Woman, behold thy son! . . . Behold thy mother!" (19:26,27). It is a place of responsibility. When we come to the cross through faith in Jesus Christ, we cannot run away, we cannot hide. We must stand there identified with Him in the fellowship of His sufferings. Then we must go away to do the work He has called us to do.

Whatever God has called you to do, my friend, do it. If you will come near the cross, you will discover what a wonderful place it really is!

Chapter 4
"Why Hast Thou Forsaken Me?"

The first three statements from our Lord on the cross really do not surprise us. You will recall that He prayed, "Father, forgive them; for they know not what they do" (Luke 23:34). He taught forgiveness, and He came to bring forgiveness; so we are not surprised at these words. When He spoke to the thief, He said, "To day shalt thou be with me in paradise" (v. 43). We expect these words, because He came that we might be forgiven and one day go to heaven. When He spoke to Mary and to the Apostle John, this does not surprise us. Our Lord fully obeyed the Law. The fifth commandment tells us to honor our father and our mother, and certainly He did this in His life and in His death. So the first three statements from the cross do not surprise us.

But the fourth statement introduces mystery. "Now from the sixth hour there was darkness over all the land unto the ninth hour. And about the ninth hour Jesus cried with a loud voice, saying, Eli, Eli, lama sabachthani? that is to say, My God, my God, why hast thou forsaken me? Some of them that stood there, when they heard that, said, This man calleth for Elias. And straightway one of them ran, and took a spunge, and filled it with vinegar, and put it on a reed, and gave him to drink. The rest said, Let be, let us see whether Elias will come to save him" (Matt. 27:45-49).

A Great Mystery

Three mysteries are wrapped up in this statement from the cross. If we understand something of these mysteries, I think we can better understand what Jesus did for us. We begin with a great mystery—the darkness around the cross. From noon until three o'clock in the afternoon, darkness was over all the land. This was a supernatural darkness. This was not a sandstorm, it was not an eclipse. (It is most unlikely that there would be an eclipse during the Passover season.) This darkness was not something that people imagined. It was a supernatural darkness sent by God the Father. What kind of a darkness was it? Why did it come?

Darkness of Sympathy

I would like to suggest three answers to that question. First of all, I think it was the darkness of sympathy. The Creator was dying on the cross, and all of creation was suffering with the Creator. We sing,

> Well might the sun in darkness hide
> And shut his glories in,
> When Christ, the mighty Maker, died
> For man the creature's sin.

We have to remember that when the first man and woman sinned, what they did affected all of creation. God forgave their sin, but He could not deliver them from the sad consequences of their sin, consequences we experience even today. Adam had to sweat for his daily bread. The toil of life is a consequence of sin. He told the woman that she would conceive and bear children in pain and in suffering. As the man tilled the ground, there would come forth thorns and briars. Death came on the scene! All of creation is suffering because of man's sin.

Everything in creation obeys God except man. God tells the rain where to fall, and the rain obeys. God tells the wind to blow, and it obeys. God tells man what to do and what not to do, and man disobeys. Yet creation is subject to vanity *because of man's sin!* According to Romans 8, all of creation is groaning and travailing in pain together. Why? It is awaiting the coming of the Creator who will set creation free. I think that this darkness is the darkness of sympathy—all of creation was sympathizing with the Creator.

When Jesus died, He did redeem creation. Man took thorns and made a crown and put that crown upon His head as they mocked Him. But really, that crown of thorns was symbolic of what He did. He took our sins to the cross. He bore them in His body on the tree. He has broken the power of sin. As a consequence, one day creation shall be delivered. One day the King shall reign, and there will be no more thorns and thistles or death and disease. It was the darkness of sympathy—creation, as it were, wrapped darkness around the Creator when He died for our sins.

Darkness of Solemnity

Second, I think that this darkness at the cross was the darkness of solemnity. The just died for the unjust. The innocent Lamb of God died for guilty sinners. I remember that in the Book of Exodus there was a great darkness. The ninth plague that God sent to Egypt was three days of darkness, a darkness so thick it could almost be felt. There was darkness over Egypt before that final judgment of the Passover and the death of the firstborn.

Behold the Lord Jesus Christ in three hours of darkness! I wonder if God was not saying that this was an hour of solemn judgment. "Now is the judgment of this world," said Jesus. "Now shall the prince of this world be cast out. And I, if I be lifted up from the earth, will draw all men unto me" (John 12:31,32). Our Lord's death on the cross was a very solemn, serious, holy event. The darkness of solemnity—the Lamb dying for our sins.

I would remind you that in the Bible "outer darkness" is a name for hell. I know some people don't like us to talk about hell. I've received mail from people who have tried to tell me that the Word of God does not teach such a thing as hell. Believe me, if we could find in the Scriptures any indication that lost sinners do not go to hell, we'd tell you about it,

45

but we haven't found it. Jesus warned about "outer darkness," and we must warn as well.

Some people have the idea that hell is just "heaven with the lights turned out." They think that there will be friendship and fellowship in hell. My friend, I would remind you that this darkness was the darkness of solemnity—the Lord Jesus died for us. Hell is no joke!

Darkness of Secrecy

Third, it was the darkness of secrecy. In those three hours Jesus Christ was accomplishing a great work that He alone could accomplish. You will recall that on the Day of Atonement, when the high priest went into the tabernacle or the temple, he went in alone. He carried on that transaction with God alone. When Jesus Christ was on the cross during those three hours of darkness, He was carrying on an eternal transaction with His Father—He finished the work that He came to do. He said in His prayer, "I have finished the work which thou gavest me to do" (John 17:4). What was that work? The work of salvation, which He alone could accomplish. He was silent for three hours, and then He spoke and said, "My God, my God, why hast thou forsaken me?" (Matt. 27:46). This was a great mystery—the darkness around the cross.

A Greater Mystery

But there is a greater mystery—the loneliness on the cross. The Lord Jesus Christ gradually moved

46

into loneliness during His final hours on earth. He went with His 12 apostles into the upper room. Judas left and only 11 were with Him. He took the 11 to the Garden of Gethsemane; three entered into the garden with Him, and they went to sleep! Then Peter and John went into the courtyard, where Peter denied Him. And then they *all* forsook Him and fled. He was left alone!

Men forsook Him, but the Father was with Him. Jesus had said in John 8:29, "And he that sent me is with me: the Father hath not left me alone; for I do always those things that please him." In John 16:32 He said, "Behold, the hour cometh, yea, is now come, that ye shall be scattered, every man to his own, and shall leave me alone: and yet I am not alone, because the Father is with me." *But at the cross the Father left Him!* The loneliness of the Saviour on the cross.

Why was He lonely? Why was He forsaken of the Father? That is what sin does—sin isolates. Sin separates man from God. Sin separates man from man. Sin separates a man from himself. You recall that the Prodigal Son "came to himself" (Luke 15:17). Sin separates a man from God. When Adam and Eve sinned, they ran and hid themselves because of the loneliness of sin.

God has never forsaken you. You may have felt as though God abandoned you, but God has never forsaken you. If God forsook you for one second, you would die, because "in him we live, and move, and have our being" (Acts 17:28). God was with Joseph in his trials, He was with Daniel, He was with

47

David, but His own Son was forsaken. Why? *He was forsaken of the Father that we might never be forsaken of the Father!* He went through darkness that we might have light. He went through isolation for us. That is what hell is—eternal loneliness, eternal isolation. There is no friendship in hell. There is no fellowship in the darkness of hell. We sense a great mystery here—the darkness around the cross. And a greater mystery—the loneliness on the cross.

The Greatest Mystery

But I think the greatest mystery of all that is identified with this statement is the blindness before the cross.

There were many people—the soldiers and others—before the cross. They heard His cry, "My God, my God, why hast thou forsaken me?" (Matt. 27:46). But they were blind. They said, "He's calling for Elijah" (see v. 47). Someone said, "Let's wait to see if Elijah comes" (see v. 49). He wasn't calling for Elijah; He was quoting Psalm 22:1. If these people had not been blind to the Scriptures, they would have recognized Psalm 22:1: "My God, my God, why hast thou forsaken me?" Also Psalm 22:2: "I cry in the daytime, but thou hearest not; and in the night season, and am not silent." There you have the darkness and the light, but the people did not recognize it. Verses 7 and 8 of Psalm 22 say, "All they that see me laugh me to scorn: they shoot out the lip, they shake the head, saying, He trusted on the Lord that he would deliver him: let him deliver
48

him, seeing he delighted in him." Psalm 22:18 says, "They part my garments among them, and cast lots upon my vesture." They did not recognize the fulfillment of prophecy before their very eyes!

What blindness! They were blind to the Scriptures, blind to the Saviour, blind to their own sin. They said, "Let's see whether Elijah will come and take him down." At that hour the Lord Jesus Christ was made sin for us, and when He was made sin, He was forsaken of the Father. We can't explain it, we don't know all that was involved in it, but we know that it is true.

There's a great mystery here—the darkness at the cross. There's a greater mystery—the loneliness on the cross. But the greatest mystery of all is the blindness before the cross.

I trust you are not blind today but that, by faith, you have seen the Lamb of God who died for you. Perhaps you have read some of the short stories written by O. Henry. When he was dying, he made this statement: "Turn up the lights—I don't want to go home in the dark." No Christian ever goes home in the dark, for "the path of the just is as the shining light, that shineth more and more unto the perfect day" (Prov. 4:18).

Let the light of the glorious gospel shine in your heart!

Chapter 5
"I Thirst"

As we listen to the Lord Jesus speak from Calvary, we certainly have no question that He loves us. This love is revealed in a special way in His fifth statement: "After this, Jesus knowing that all things were now accomplished, that the scripture might be fulfilled, saith, I thirst. Now there was set a vessel full of vinegar: and they filled a spunge with vinegar, and put it upon hyssop, and put it to his mouth. When Jesus therefore had received the vinegar, he said, It is finished: and he bowed his head, and gave up the ghost [spirit]" (John 19:28-30).

Our Lord was crucified at nine o'clock in the morning, and He spent the first three hours on the cross in the sunlight. Then the darkness came, and at the end of that darkness, He cried, "My God, my God, why hast thou forsaken me?" (Matt. 27:46). His last three statements from the cross centered upon Himself. His first three statements centered upon others—His enemies, the thief, and John and Mary. But in the last three statements our Lord focused upon Himself: His body—"I thirst" (John 19:28); His soul—"It is finished" (v. 30; Isa. 53:10); His spirit—"Father, into thy hands I commend my spirit" (Luke 23:46). Body, soul and spirit—all were offered by the Lord Jesus Christ in perfect obedience to His Father.

The shortest of all the statements that our Lord made from the cross is the one found in John 19:28: "I thirst." In the Greek New Testament it is one word of four letters. It is the only statement in which our Lord referred to His body and His physical suffering. This simple word reveals to us the heart of the Lord Jesus, and we see His love in a deeper way.

Let me put it this way. When I hear the Lord Jesus say, "I thirst," I see three portraits of Christ: I see the suffering Son of Man, the obedient servant of God and the loving Saviour of sinners.

The Suffering Son of Man

Let's look at the first portrait, the suffering Son of Man. Jesus Christ was truly man, so don't ever deny His humanity. Liberal theologians today deny His deity, but in the early church there was no question about the deity of Christ. There were those who questioned His humanity and who said that He really was not a man. They said that He just appeared to be a man. This is one reason why I John was written—to reaffirm once again the fact that Jesus Christ was truly man as well as truly God.

Jesus was born as a baby. He grew up as a child and a youth. He ate and drank. He became weary. He had to sleep. He felt pain. He wept. And He died. All of these experiences belong to humanity. They are the sinless experiences of humanity. Our Lord Jesus was "holy, harmless, undefiled" (Heb. 7:26)—

perfect man. He never exhibited in any way any kind of sin, for He was sinless. However, He did participate in the sinless infirmities of human nature.

When our Lord Jesus was on the cross, He felt the depths of suffering—physical suffering and spiritual suffering. When he came to Calvary, He was offered the same narcotic that the two thieves were offered. Apparently they partook of it; He did not. He refused to drink the wine that was mingled with myrrh because He did not want His senses to be stupefied in any way. Our Lord Jesus Christ, when He died on the cross, was in perfect control of His faculties; He did not seek to escape pain in any way.

The high priest in the Old Testament, when he was ministering in the tabernacle or the temple, was warned not to drink strong drink. When our Lord Jesus Christ offered Himself as the sacrifice for sin, He did not want in any way to be identified with strong drink—He was in full control of Himself. He was the suffering Son of Man.

Do you know what this means for us today? It means that Jesus Christ is able to empathize completely with us, to identify with our pain and our need and our hurt. I am not suggesting that it is wrong for us today to have anesthesia when we have surgery. After all, when God performed the first surgery on Adam, He did put him to sleep. I am suggesting, however, that our Lord Jesus Christ, to become our merciful High Priest, endured that suffering and paid the full price. Therefore, we are able to come boldly to the throne of grace (see Heb. 4:16). We are able to come to One who understands just how much we hurt, just how we feel. He knows the burdens we are carrying and the pain we are enduring.

Wherever I go, I find people who are hurting. There is physical pain, there is emotional pain, there are spiritual burdens and battles. My Lord, the suffering Son of Man, who cried, "I thirst," has identified Himself with our every need. That encourages me to pray. That encourages me to keep on going. That encourages me not to quit, because I can come at any time to the throne of grace and find grace to help in the time of need. The first portrait we see in the words "I thirst" is that of the suffering Son of Man.

The Obedient Servant of God

The second portrait is of the obedient servant of God. Why did Jesus say, "I thirst"? (John 19:28). That the Scripture might be fulfilled. He obeyed completely the Word of God. In fact, everything our Lord did was in obedience to the Word of God. Our Lord fulfilled the Word in Psalm 69:21: "They gave me also gall for my meat; and in my thirst they gave me vinegar to drink." Our Lord Jesus was obeying the Word of God.

We are not surprised that the Lord Jesus thirsted. Crucifixion is an agonizing form of death. As a person hangs on the cross, all of his physical juices are drained right out of him. Psalm 69 talks about this when it describes His sufferings: "Reproach hath broken my heart; I am full of heaviness: and I looked for some to take pity, but there was none; and for comforters, but I found none" (v. 20). "My throat is dried: mine eyes fail while I wait for my God" (v. 3). You can read Psalm 69 and discover a portrait of our suffering Saviour, the obedient servant of God.

He said, "My meat is to do the will of him that sent me, and to finish his work" (John 4:34). When I hear the Lord Jesus say, "I thirst," it reminds me that I must be obedient to the Word of God. You have noticed, I'm sure, how many times in the Gospel of Matthew we read the words: "And this he said [or did] that it might be fulfilled which was spoken by the prophet." Why was He born in Bethlehem? It fulfilled prophecy. Why did He go down to Egypt? It fulfilled prophecy. Why did our Lord move to Nazareth? It fulfilled prophecy. Why did He do what He did? He was obeying the Word of God. "Obedient unto death, even the death of the cross" (Phil. 2:8). He was the obedient servant of God. The most important thing in the life of the believer is to know the will of God and do it. "Doing the will of God from the heart," says Ephesians 6:6.

The Loving Saviour of Sinners

We have seen two portraits of the Lord Jesus in this statement: the suffering Son of Man and the obedient servant of God. Now notice the third portrait—the loving Saviour of sinners.

Jesus was thirsty, to be sure, because of the physical agony He was experiencing. But I would remind you that He had just come through those three hours of darkness when the sun had veiled its face. Jesus Christ, in that time of darkness, had cried, "My God, my God, why hast thou forsaken me?" (Matt. 27:46). I would like to suggest to you that when the Lord Jesus was made sin, when He completed that great transaction for our salvation, He endured our hell for us. Hell is a place of thirst. In Luke 16, our Lord told about a man who died and woke up in the place of judgment, and in that place of judgment, he was thirsty. People in that place of judgment are saying, "I thirst." When my Lord died for me and was made sin for me, He thirsted.

I would suggest to you that hell is a place of eternal thirst, where people will thirst endlessly and will not be able to be satisfied. They will thirst for reality and satisfaction, but their thirst will not be quenched.

Please notice that there were several cups at Calvary. There was the cup of *charity*—they offered Him wine mingled with myrrh, an opiate to deaden His pain, but He rejected it (see Mark 15:23). There was the cup of *mockery*—the soldiers offered Him sour wine (see Luke 23:36). There was the cup of *sympathy*—somebody put some vinegar on a sponge and lifted it to His dry lips (see John 19:29). But the greatest cup of all was the cup of *iniquity*. He said in the Garden, "The cup which my Father hath given me, shall I not drink of it?" (18:11).

Have you ever traced the word "water" in the Gospel of John? In John 2, our Lord turned water into wine. They ran out of wine, because everything

55

the world has eventually runs out. The world cannot supply what you need. Only Jesus can. In John 4, Jesus said to that woman at the well, "If you drink of this water, you'll thirst again; if you drink of the water that I'm going to give you, you'll never thirst" (see vv. 13,14). Sin never quenches thirst; it makes the desire even stronger, but the satisfaction is weaker. In John 7, at the Feast of Tabernacles, our Lord cried out, "If any man thirst, let him come unto me, and drink" (v. 37). He was referring to that rock in the Old Testament that was smitten that the waters might flow forth (see Ex. 17:6). He was smitten on the cross that we might have the water of life.

There is no thirst in heaven. Revelation 7:16 says, "They shall hunger no more, neither thirst any more." In fact, Revelation 22:17 (the last invitation in the Bible) invites all who thirst to come and "take the water of life freely." The question today is not, "Do you thirst?" because all mankind has a thirst for reality, a thirst for God, a thirst for forgiveness. The real question is "How long are you going to thirst?" When you trust Jesus Christ as your Saviour, you will never thirst again.

I was having dinner one evening with a preacher friend of mine. As so often happens in restaurants, the waitress came and asked, "Would you like something from the bar?" My friend very tenderly said, "Honey, over 20 years ago I took a drink, and I haven't been thirsty since." Then he told her about the Lord Jesus who satisfies all thirst.

The Lord Jesus Christ thirsted on the cross that we might never thirst again. He is the suffering Son of Man, He is the obedient servant of God, He is the loving Saviour of sinners. When you put your faith and trust in Him, He will satisfy you, and you will never thirst again.

Chapter 6
"It Is Finished"

We today do not like to face the horror of the cross. We have embellished the cross. We have almost beautified it. We have made the cross into a piece of jewelry. But you must remember that crucifixion meant shame, torture and a slow and agonizing death. Our Lord Jesus was "obedient unto death, even the death of the cross" (Phil. 2:8).

The sixth word from the cross is recorded in John 19:30: "When Jesus therefore had received the vinegar, he said, It is finished: and he bowed his head, and gave up the ghost [spirit]." When you compare the Gospel records, you discover that He shouted this statement. With a loud voice He cried, "It is finished." Then He bowed His head, and He gave up His spirit.

At the age of 33 most people are saying, "It is beginning." But at the age of about 33 Jesus was saying, "It is finished!" He did not say, "I am finished." It was not a cry of defeat; it was a shout of victory. In the Greek language in which John wrote, this statement was one word with ten letters— *tetelestai*. Perhaps that is a new word to you. It means "it is finished, it stands finished, and it always will be finished."

I must confess to you that many of the things I

have started, I have never finished. I have book manuscripts in my file that I have never completed. But our Lord Jesus Christ was able at the end of His ministry to shout in great victory, "It is finished." Because of this, you and I have the assurance of eternal salvation.

A Familiar Word

Consider with me three important facts about this word that our Lord uttered—"It is finished" (John 19:30). First of all, it was a familiar word. *Tetelestai* is certainly not a familiar word to us today, but it was a familiar word in our Lord's time. The archaeologists have dug up many ancient Greek documents that help us better understand the Bible. People used to think that the Greek of the New Testament was a special "holy language." Now we know that the Greek of the New Testament was the common language of the people of that day. This word, "It is finished"—*tetelestai*—does not belong to some heavenly vocabulary, although it certainly has a wonderful heavenly meaning. It was a familiar word.

Servants

If you were to check the Greek lexicons, you would find that the servants and the slaves used this word. A master would tell his servant to go do something, and when the servant had completed the task, he would come back and say, "*Tetelestai*— I have finished the work that you gave me to do."

The Lord Jesus Christ was God's suffering servant. Philippians 2 informs us that Jesus Christ came as a servant. He did not come as a sovereign but as a servant, not as a ruler but as a slave. The Lord Jesus Christ had a work to do. He said in John 17:4, "I have finished the work which thou gavest me to do."

Priests

You will discover that the priests also used this word. The Jewish people had to bring their sacrifices to the priest to be examined, because it was against the law to offer an imperfect sacrifice at the altar of God. After the priest had examined the sacrifice, he would say, "It is perfect." (Of course, he would use the Hebrew or the Aramaic word, but it would be the equivalent of *tetelestai.*)

Jesus Christ, dying on the cross, was God's perfect, faultless sacrifice—the Lamb of God who takes away the sin of the world. How do we know Christ is a faultless sacrifice? God the Father said that He is. When the Lord Jesus was baptized, God the Father spoke from heaven and said, "This is my beloved Son, in whom I am well pleased" (Matt. 3:17). God the Father put His seal of approval upon God the Son, and God the Holy Spirit came down as a dove and added His witness (see v. 16). Even the demons admitted that Jesus was the Son of God (see 8:28,29). His enemies had to admit that He was faultless, because they had to hire liars to bear false witness against Him. His followers found no fault in Him. None of the apostles ever said, "We heard Jesus tell a lie" or, "We saw Jesus do something wrong." He is the spotless, perfect sacrifice.

Pilate said, "I find no fault in this man" (Luke 23:4). Even Judas said, "I have betrayed innocent blood" (Matt. 27:4). *Tetelestai!* The priests used this word; it means "a perfect, faultless sacrifice." You will not find any other sacrifice for your sins who is perfect, spotless and faultless. Jesus Christ is the only one.

Artists

The servants used this word, and the priests used it as well. The artists also used it. When a painter completed his work, he would step back and say, "*Tetelestai*—it is finished!" It means, "The picture is completed."

When you read the Old Testament, you have a rather difficult picture. In the Old Testament are ceremonies, types, prophecies and some mysterious symbols. Even those of us who have been studying the Word of God for many years often find serious difficulties as we study the Old Testament Scriptures. The Old Testament was God's picture gallery in the shadows. So many Old Testament passages seem incomplete and hard to understand. When Jesus Christ came, He completed the picture and turned on the light! He is God's wonderful completion to the Old Testament revelation.

I like that scene in Luke 24 where those two discouraged men were walking on the road to

Emmaus. A stranger joined them, and they told him about the death of the Lord Jesus. (Can you imagine telling Jesus about His own death?) Jesus said to them, "O fools, and slow of heart to believe all that the prophets have spoken" (v. 25). Beginning at Moses and all the prophets, the Lord Jesus went through the Old Testament Scriptures and explained the total picture. Calvary completed the picture. *Tetelestai*—it is finished!

We today read the Old Testament, and even though there are some difficulties and some things that are hard to understand, because we know Christ, the light is shining. The portraits are no longer in the shadows; we can see the complete picture that God has painted.

Merchants

It was a familiar word. The slaves used it, the priests used it, and the artists used it. The merchants also used it. To them, it meant "the debt is fully paid." If you had purchased something, the merchant would take your money and then would give you a receipt. That receipt would say "*Tetelestai*—it is finished." The debt had been fully paid.

You and I as sinners are in debt before God, and we cannot pay this debt. We have broken God's law, and we are bankrupt. The wages of sin is death. But Jesus came and paid the debt for us. That is what *tetelestai* means. It was a familiar word. The servant had finished the work. The perfect sacrifice had been offered. The picture had been completed. The debt had been paid.

A Faithful Saviour

Fact number two: It was a familiar word shouted by a faithful Saviour. He came to do a great work, the work of salvation. When he was 12 years old, Jesus said, "I must be about my Father's business" (Luke 2:49). In John 2:4, at the wedding in Cana, He said, "Mine hour is not yet come." In John 4:34 He said, "My meat is to do the will of him that sent me, and to finish his work." On the Mount of Transfiguration, our Lord discussed with Moses and Elijah His "decease that he should accomplish at Jerusalem" (Luke 9:31). One day He said to His disciples, "I have a baptism to be baptized with; and how I am straitened till it be accomplished!" (12:50). In His high-priestly prayer He said, "I have glorified thee on the earth: I have finished the work which thou gavest me to do" (John 17:4). *Tetelestai* was a familiar word spoken by a faithful Saviour. I am glad that He was faithful to do the work that God gave Him to do.

A Finished Work

That leads us to the third fact: It was a familiar word spoken by a faithful Saviour about a finished work. All of the prophecies that referred to Him and His work on the cross were finished. Beginning in Genesis 3:15, God had promised that a Saviour would come and defeat Satan. All of the pictures in the tabernacle, the priesthood, the sacrifices, the furnishings—all of these were completely finished and fulfilled. The types and prophecies were finished. The veil of the temple was torn in two, and man was able to enter in. God had opened the way of salvation!

This also means that the Law is finished. Some people are afraid of this truth, but it is there in the Scriptures. Colossians 2:14 says, "Blotting out the handwriting of ordinances that was against us, which was contrary to us, and took it out of the way, nailing it to his cross." The righteousness of the Law was fulfilled through the finished work of Jesus Christ. God the Father upheld His own holiness and yet fulfilled His own demands when Jesus died on the cross. There is therefore now no condemnation to them that are in Christ Jesus" (Rom. 8:1). The types and prophecies are finished, and the Law is finished. All of which means the work of salvation is finished! The great word of the gospel is not "do," it is "done." The work has been finished!

Some years ago there was an eccentric evangelist whose name was Alexander Wooton. A man came to him one day and said, rather sarcastically, "What must I do to be saved?" Knowing the man was not serious, Wooton replied, "It's too late!" The man became alarmed. He said, "No, no, what must I do to be saved?" And Wooton said, "It's too late! It's already been done!" That is the message of the gospel—the work of salvation is completed. It is finished!

The Book of Hebrews explains this completed salvation: "Once in the end of the world [age] hath he appeared to put away sin by the sacrifice of himself. And as it is appointed unto men once to die, but after this the judgment: So Christ was once offered to bear the sins of many. . . . It is not possible that the blood of bulls and of goats should take away sin. . . . But this man, after he had offered one sacrifice for sins for ever, sat down on the right hand of God" (Heb. 9:26-28; 10:4,12). The work of salvation is completed. "It is finished" (John 19:30). Our Lord was buried. He arose from the dead. He returned to glory, and He sat down because the work was finished. In the Old Testament tabernacle there were no chairs because the work of the priest was never finished. But Jesus Christ sat down—His work had been finished.

Since salvation is a finished work, we dare not add anything to it or take anything from it or substitute anything for it. There is only one way of salvation—it is faith in the finished work of the Lord Jesus Christ. When my Lord died, He cried, *"Tetelestai*—it is finished!"* It was a familiar word shouted by a faithful Saviour about a finished work.

> Lifted up was He to die,
> 'It is finished,' was His cry;
> Now in heav'n exalted high:
> Hallelujah, what a Savior!

Is He *your* Saviour?

Chapter 7
"Into Thy Hands I Commend My Spirit"

You are not really prepared to live unless you are prepared to die. Much of what goes on in this world is a battle against death. Death is going to come. It is an appointment, and only God knows the hour. That is why it is wonderful to be a Christian, to know Jesus as your Saviour. You then have confidence and do not have to worry about death. Jesus' seventh statement from the cross tells us about death and how He died.

"And when Jesus had cried with a loud voice, he said, Father, into thy hands I commend my spirit: and having said thus, he gave up the ghost" (Luke 23:46). Four characteristics of His death should encourage us and take away any fear of death.

He Died Actually

First of all, He died actually. His death was not an illusion; He actually died. The Lord Jesus had a real human body, and He experienced all of the sinless infirmities of human nature. He knew what it was to grow up; He knew what it was to eat, drink and sleep. And our Lord Jesus knew what it was to die. He died actually. His death was a real death.

John recorded that the officials checked very

carefully to be sure that Jesus had died. When the soldiers came to look at the bodies on the crosses, they discovered that Jesus already was dead (see John 19:33). Therefore, they did not break His legs. When Joseph and Nicodemus wanted to get custody of the body of Jesus to give it a decent burial, they had to check with Pilate, and Pilate marveled that Jesus was already dead (Mark 15:44). The official evidence of the Roman Empire was that Jesus actually had died.

The evidence of the gospel writers is that He actually died. He did not swoon on the cross and then, when he was put into the cool tomb, revive and pretend it was a resurrection. That kind of foolish religious thinking went out a long time ago. The Lord Jesus Christ died actually; He tasted death for every person.

In the Bible the word "death" is applied to believers very infrequently. It's called "sleep." Christians who die are those who "sleep in Jesus" (I Thess. 4:14). But when Jesus died, it was not sleep—it was death. He tasted the full experience of death. He confronted the last enemy—death—and courageously faced its sorrow, its trial, its pain, its finality. He died actually. When you stop to think that He died for us, that means that we do not have to be afraid of death.

He Died Confidently

This fact leads to the second characteristic of my Lord's death: He not only died actually, He also died

67

confidently. He said, "Father, into thy hands I commend my spirit" (Luke 23:46).

The Father's Presence

He died confidently because He had the Father's presence. He said, "Father." Three times on the cross, Jesus addressed God: His first word from the cross was "Father, forgive them; for they know not what they do" (Luke 23:34); His fourth word was "My God, my God, why hast thou forsaken me?" (Matt. 27:46). His seventh word was "Father, into thy hands I commend my spirit" (Luke 23:46). At the beginning, in the middle and at the end of His ordeal, our Lord prayed to His Father.

It is worth noting that the word "Father" was often on our Lord's lips. When He was 12 years old, He said, "Wist ye not [don't you know] that I must be about my Father's business?" (2:49). In the Sermon on the Mount, He used the word "Father" more than 15 times. In the upper room discourse and in His high-priestly prayer (John 17) our Lord talked about the Father many times. He died confidently—He had the Father's presence.

The Father's Promise

He died confidently because He had the Father's promise. Our Lord quoted part of Psalm 31:5: "Into thine hand I commit my spirit: thou hast redeemed me, O Lord God of truth." Psalm 31:5 is an Old Testament promise, and Jesus applied it to Himself.

But he changed it, and since He is the author of the Word, He can do this. He added the word "Father," but He omitted the phrase about being redeemed: "Thou hast redeemed me, O Lord God of truth." Jesus did not have to be redeemed. He had never sinned, and it was not necessary for Him to be redeemed. When He died, He claimed God's Word and entrusted Himself to the Father.

All three of the prayers from the cross are tied to Scripture. When Jesus prayed, "Father, forgive them; for they know not what they do" (Luke 23:34), He was fulfilling Isaiah 53:12: "He . . . made intercession for the transgressors." When He cried out, "My God, my God, why hast thou forsaken me" (Matt. 27:46), He was quoting Psalm 22:1. When He said, "Father, into thy hands I commend my spirit" (Luke 23:46), He fulfilled Psalm 31:5. Our Lord Jesus lived by God's Word, and if you *live* by God's Word, you can *die* by God's Word. What assurance do you have that you will experience confidence in death? The only assurance we have is the Word of God. He died confidently with the Father's presence and with the Father's promise.

The Father's Protection

Third, He had the Father's protection. "Into thy hands I commend my spirit" (Luke 23:46). For many hours our Lord had been in the hands of sinners. He had told His disciples, "I'm going to be delivered into the hands of sinners." The hands of sinners took hold of Him and bound Him. The hands of sinners beat Him. The hands of sinners stripped Him. The hands of sinners put a crown of thorns upon His head. The hands of sinners nailed Him to a cross. But when He came to the conclusion of His work, Jesus Christ was no longer in the hands of sinners; He was in the Father's hands. He died confidently because He was in the Father's hands. "[Thou] hast not shut me up into the hand of the enemy" (Ps. 31:8). And Psalm 31:15 says, "My times are in thy hand: deliver me from the hand of mine enemies, and from them that persecute me." The greatest safety is in the Father's hands.

He Died Willingly

He died actually, and He died confidently. He also died willingly. In one sense, our Lord was killed. Peter said, "Him . . . ye have taken, and by wicked hands have crucified and slain" (Acts 2:23). But in another sense, He was not killed, for He willingly laid down His life. He said, "Therefore doth my Father love me, because I lay down my life, that I might take it again. No man taketh it from me, but I lay it down of myself. I have power [authority] to lay it down, and I have power to take it again" (John 10:17,18). Our Lord Jesus Christ died willingly.

This is an amazing thing! No Old Testament sacrifice ever died willingly. No lamb, goat or sheep ever willingly gave its life. But Jesus willingly laid down His life for us. It is a wonderful thing to be able to say, "Father, into thy hands I commend my spirit." He died actually, He died confidently, and He died willingly.

Before Jesus Christ laid down His life, He forgave His enemies. Before He laid down His life, He gave salvation to a repenting thief. Before He laid down His life, He cared for His mother. Before He laid down His life, He finished the work God gave Him to do. You and I do not know how long God is going to permit us to live. Every day we have, every minute we have, is a gift of His grace. But today we ought to forgive our enemies—just in case we should die. We do not want to die with anything in our hearts against anybody. We want to come to the time of death having shared salvation with others. We want to be faithful in taking care of those who depend upon us. We want to be able to come to the end of life and surrender to God willingly, having finished the work God wants us to do.

He Died Victoriously

He died actually, He died confidently, and He died willingly; finally, He died victoriously. He cried out, "Father, into thy hands I commend my spirit" (Luke 23:46). Our Lord Jesus Christ accomplished the work that God gave Him to do, and when He gave up His spirit, several miracles took place. The veil of the temple was torn from top to bottom, and God opened the way into the Holy of Holies (see Matt. 27:51). Some graves were opened, and some of the saints were resurrected (v. 52). Jesus Christ proved Himself to be victorious over sin (the torn

71

veil) and over death (the opened graves). There was even an earthquake that shook the area! (v. 51). It reminds us of the earthquake at Mount Sinai when God came down and gave the Law (see Ex. 19:18). But this earthquake did not announce the terror of the Law. It announced the fulfillment of the Law! The Lord Jesus Christ died victoriously, conqueror of sin, death and hell!

The Lord Jesus Christ died for sinners. He died actually, He died confidently, He died willingly, and He died victoriously. He did not die for His own sin because He had none. He died for the sins of the world. Someday you are going to die. Usually people die just the way they lived. To be sure, God can work and people can be saved at the last minute. I have led people on their deathbeds to Christ. *But don't take that chance.* Don't gamble with eternity.

You can die confidently, with the assurance that you are going to the Father's house. You can die with the promises of God's Word to give you grace and strength and comfort. You can die in the safest place in all of the universe—in the hand of God. Jesus said, "My sheep hear my voice, and I know them, and they follow me: And I give unto them eternal life; and they shall never perish, neither shall any man pluck them out of my hand" (John 10:27,28). What a wonderful thing it is to die with confidence and assurance, able to say, "Father, into thy hands I commend my spirit."